# LITTLE GIRL LOST, WOMAN FOUND

TAMERA WISE

KNOTTED ROAD PRESS, INC.

*I'd like to dedicate this book to my daughter Aleah who with her life showed me the importance of mine and what REAL love meant.*
*And to my loving wonderful husband Richard Allen Wise for showing me such unwavering, unconditional love always.*

1

## RAD

OK so you're probably reading this thinking RAD is the first name of the first chapter. That seems odd, but in this instance RAD means: Reactive Attachment Disorder. This is one of many diagnoses I have been given over the many years of therapy, including GAD, Generalized Anxiety Disorder, PTSD, Post-Traumatic Stress Disorder, OCD-Obsessive Compulsive Disorder, Major Depression, Adjustment Disorder, need I say more?

So it seemed fitting to me that this be where my story starts.

I was conceived by parents that I'm not sure loved each other, certainly didn't trust each other and probably didn't expect or want to have me. I have a biological brother 2 yrs 9 months older than I, paternity never questioned, lovingly reared and accepted. But by the time I came the waters were murky; deceit, infidelity and distrust deep seated in the lives of Worley James and Carol Marie.

I guess under those circumstances, what happened was bound and determined to, as they wouldn't have me for very long.

They split just a few months after I was born and at nine months old I was placed in the care of a family member to fostered.

From approximately nine months old to two and a half years

I lived with my biological brother in the home of an aunt who already had six children of her own.

I was an infant child so obviously I don't remember much but what I do remember is the lack of affection, attention, love and reassurance, or a natural sense of being cared for. This is where RAD came from.

Some of the other things I do remember are the taste of warm goats milk, never enough to eat, being the smallest of all the kids (unnoticed as it were) and seemingly always in just a diaper, dirty head to toe.

I've been told that my biological parents visited me, but I don't recall that, I don't remember visits or feeling loved or being given affection. And many years later I came to understand that they were immersed in a very ugly divorce and custody battle that Worley James ultimately won.

It's important to mention that "Winning" was important at all costs. Not because there was so much love but no one wanted to lose.

Both my father and Carol Marie during this time found new mates, ultimately marrying and in Carol's case starting a new family almost immediately.

Of course, I didn't know until many years later exactly how these first formidable years of my life would affect me long-term, but oh how they affected me long-term.

I suppose those two and a half years were basically the foundation of how the rest of my life would be: feeling that I was never enough, needing validation, craving attention, fear of being abandoned, and so much more.

But as the saying states, Life goes on, and that it did.

Fasten your seatbelts it is going to be a bumpy ride...

# THIS SO-CALLED FAMILY LIFE

Well it should go without saying that at two and a half years old I don't always have real clear recollection of what happened, but based on the subsequent reading of court documents and other information gathered I'll do my best to re-create the events.

So as I understand it, while I was in foster care from nine months of age until this time in my life, two and a half years old, my parents were in a pretty nasty custody battle one that ranged anywhere from my father trying to convince my mother to split the children him taking my brother and my mother taking me which was not agreed to and ultimately forcing the judge to say that neither of the parents were fit at the time which forced us both into foster care.

After that they both entered into new relationships, my biological mother much faster than my father, she remarried and became pregnant and my father met and married my stepmother and ultimately they ended up winning full custody of both my brother and I, me now 2 ½ yrs old.

This stage of life starts in the town of Riverside, California on a street named Artesian.

Even though my father had other family we never spent much time with them, if any at all, even the sister who fostered us for almost 2 years.

If I'm being completely honest I didn't spend much time with my father at all.

Which left the time spent with my stepmother's family: her mom and dad and sister who all lived in a house in downtown Riverside.

And another sister and her husband and their two children who lived up in Northern California but visited during summers and holidays.

It was a time of very mixed emotions. Living with complete strangers most of whom I assume wanted to create happiness in raising small children, but there was a Darkside to this change.

The Darkside consisted of a child molester, emotional and physical neglect and an ongoing lack of understanding for children who had been traumatized at such a young age.

My stepmother's father seem to like little girls in a way that was not appropriate.

From the age of approximately two years and nine months well into my teens I was subject to all those various types of abuse from sexual molestation to emotional and other pure neglect...

So now after saying that it should be shared that I lack a lot of memory. The more vivid memories I have are those of abuse or that are negative. Fun and happy memories were and still are, few and far between.

I'm here to share my story in hopes of healing others with similar backgrounds, so with that said, it will be the good, the bad, and the ugly.

My first memory of any type of molestation was that about two years and nine months. The biological father of my stepmother was a big man, tall and heavyset.

I don't recall exactly what he did for a living but I believe it was working on the railroad or some type of factory. When he came home he always smelled of oil, grease, body odor, and often alcohol and tobacco.

When we were there visiting (I'm grateful we didn't live there full-time), and we visited often, he would always ask me to sit on his lap , I would quickly and instinctually know from the overwhelming smell which made me uncomfortable, what was likely to happen.

He would fondle me at times, just on my breasts but others in my vaginal area.

This went on for years, as many as I can remember , it was just what happened when visiting Grandmas house.

The first time it escalated from fondling to anything else I was maybe around five if my memory serves me correct.

At the grandparents' house there was an attached shed and in that shed was a second refrigerator, a meat freezer, and an area of shelving that held sundries and canned goods for storage.

Anyway on the days that we were there, usually the weekend, and ALWAYS Sunday's, I was always sent to the storage shed to get the meat out of the freezer for whatever dinner we were having. It very seldom failed that once I was inside the storage shed I would hear the cryptic sound of the lock latch closing which if you think about it why would you have a latch that you could lock from the inside of the shed???

I suppose this is why.

I don't have entirely clear memories even though I've spent years in therapy, had hypnotherapy, EMDR and other types. It always seems that when reaching the deepest memories my body literally goes into a full-blown panic attack and my mind won't let it remember exactly everything that happened what I do remember is dark and fear and shame.

I do however remember what I felt, as if it were yesterday, the fear so palatable and familiar. At least 9 years of this buried in my memory, I still get triggered by body odor smell, cigars and stale alcohol odors

The other side of visiting this home were some very happy

memories spending time with my favorite aunt Beverly swimming in the pool and always meals with very yummy food which probably started my love for food, which is a good and bad thing.

It may seem that I am all over the place when writing this and I probably am but memories come in and out there are good and there are bad.

So let's keep this going.

Pretty much every visit during my youth was filled with visits to the storage shed and the latch that closed; inappropriate touching and more, some very painful acts of sexual abuse that a child should never have to endure. At the same time combined with laughs and good food and some of the only affection I got during those years from my wonderful Aunt who never married and had her own children but treated me like her own more than anyone else.

I suppose from the beginning until probably the age of seven things went on this way before they got a little worse.

My step family also consisted of another aunt, who lived in the same state but not nearby, who would visit once or twice a year usually during the summers or holidays.

She had two children approximately the same age as my brother and I with just a few months difference between us, one being a boy and the other a girl.

What was then introduced to my life was the sexual abuse that was much different than what I was experiencing as it was basically child on child.

The male step cousin one day became very sexually aggressive. I recall him taking me out to the far end of the property where there was a large garage shed and an open car area. There was an old truck there and a fenced-in area and then along the backside was chain-link and he would take me in the very far corner behind the garage and he would take his pants down and force me to my knees and hold my head against his genitals forcing copulation.

Of course it didn't feel right but I was only 7 years old and he was 9 ½ so I couldn't comprehend it being right or wrong. I just knew that it didn't feel like something that should be done.

One time when all of this took place it just so happened that my brother and the female step cousin stepped out to the corner of the property and from inside the garage were looking through slats of wood they witnessed what was taking place.

They made noise which alerted us to their presence and of course it stopped but then a whole other situation and new abuse was born in that moment: my brother using the information he had just found out against me and shaming me at any time possible to do his chores or to just make me feel bad.

I suppose I should insert hear that my brother and I were never really close or bonded. Perhaps because we were not raised in a traditional setting or nurtured to become true siblings, what I do remember is my poor little heart breaking at knowing that not only did he not try and protect me from what was going on but would use it against me for years to his benefit and for his own will.

So again aside from the step grandfather and the step cousin inflicting their sexual abuses on me, I had my brother emotionally abusing me and at this point my parents completely neglecting me it was a hard row to tow, to say the least.

Life really takes another crazy turn when around nine years old my father and my stepmother start to have their own marital issues, (which should be told there were always marital issues as I'm not sure there was much of a marriage).

My father was never a faithful man and getting to know him the way that I did later, he clearly had little respect for women as a whole so it's probably unfortunate that my stepmother invested so much emotionally in a man who could never return those feelings, and certainly should have been more self respecting then to allow his mis-treatment.

As things got difficult between them the fights became more frequent. The yelling and the screaming in the night when he didn't come home. It was a very toxic environment for everyone.

This went on for a few years, probably three, maybe four ,my dad staying out and coming home smelling like liquor and other women.

My mom crying and calling him every name you can think of. Even tearing the house apart looking for the gun to see who would survive. Scary times.

It became clear that my brother and I would be fending for ourselves, trying to be normal, going to school, faking smiles, and trying to concentrate.

Interestingly enough my brother did very well in school. Of course he was nearly three years older than I was so perhaps he had a bit of a head start but he was always excelling at his education where I always struggled. I think from early on I was very anxious, probably depressed, and can't remember living my life any other way, every day, without fear and shame.

Fear of not having a home, a roof over my head, food in my stomach. The not knowing what kind of day it was going to be. Would it be filled full of arguing and yelling and screaming and name-calling? Would it include sexual abuse or physical abuse? Emotional abuse? One never knew from day to day.

I pause in this moment as I'm writing, wondering to myself, oh geez this book is going to be very long if I include every incident and every horrible experience during my childhood so I will try and keep on track best I can.

At around eleven I can recall, things got pretty bad. Dad wasn't coming home at all for the most part and mom was scrambling to hold her life together and hold onto him which was literally impossible.

I can remember one night him not coming home and I don't know how, but she found out where the other woman lived that he was with at the time.

At some ungodly hour of the night she put me in the car and drove over to the woman's apartment, which was upstairs I remember, and had me knock on the door and when the woman answered in her negligee, I saw my father laying on the couch with almost no clothes on, and of course the screaming ensued.

Not long after that the proceedings of separation began. I am leaving out that during this period of time my father purchased a home in another city trying to escape his marriage only for him to be sold out by the escrow company that contacted my stepmother to tell her about it while clearing title and for her to get the keys for move-in. Boy, that was an interesting situation.

Anyway, I'll fast forward to the divorce proceedings, which I don't think could've been any uglier. It was clear that my father wanted my brother but not me ( déjà vu') and my stepmom was not letting him have either one of us.

I'm not sure if it's because she really wanted us (as she was never emotionally invested in our well being) or if she did it to spite him, (I lean towards the latter), but at the end of the day the fight was for us both. After an ugly court battle, probably unprecedented back in that day, as a step-parent rarely if ever won) my stepmother was granted custody of both my brother and I.

I'm going to give a lot of credit to the lawyer and his ability to bring to light my father and his very unhealthy lifestyle. And the fact that we were brainwashed to HATE my father and actually were called in Judges Chambers to testify against him.

So we are now older and moved back to Riverside where we live in a house on the same street as the house we lived in as a family just a few doors down.

I think I am 13 going on 14 and my brother almost 16

The good news is that the step grandfather who is older, really now almost stopped inappropriate touching and his attempts at any sexual contact had waned.

Unfortunately the step cousin would still visit, and he was always up to no good as much as he could get away with, he was just as aggressive and inappropriate every time he visited.

H ome life was very difficult. There was no love in our house, mostly anger, bitterness, loneliness and sadness.

I often wondered why she fought so hard for us to only, what seemed to be, punish us for all his wrongdoings.

The one shining light was that angel of my aunt Beverly who was always there to give love and a cheeseburger and chocolate shake. Food was such a comfort and friend to me

I would not understand for many years, how depressed and unhappy I truly was. My mind always in "survival" mode, ready for whatever came next. But hoping and faithful that a silver of love and attention would shine on my day, but most commonly never did.

My stepmother worked full time but hated it, she was so resentful that she had these 2 children, that were not hers that she was responsible for. She complained about money constantly, she never had enough; life never gave her enough, she always wanted more and made everyone in her path miserable because of it. She cursed my Father on a daily basis and wished him dead.

Thinking back now I can't imagine how ones mind could keep up with the trauma of all the adult abuses so consistently and constantly compiling.

Well now into my teens obviously other worldly events start to take place.

As most troubled youth I got into the wrong crowd. As I stated previously I wasn't a good student and so commenced with what would turn out to be years of self-harm and sabotage.

It started with something as simple as sniffing paint to get high and then of course alcohol. I mean alcohol was everywhere in the 70s.

At almost fifteen I went with a friend to a house party and of course there was alcohol. At some point what I drank made me feel very funny the next thing I remember I woke up. I was naked but there was no one in the room and so I put my clothes on and went to the bathroom where I found myself bleeding. I wiped myself and proceeded to get dressed. When I walked into the living room there were a couple of people I said nothing to, then walked out the front door and found my way home. I never spoke about that day until many years later in therapy. That was my introduction to a whole other kind of abuse. First of three times I'd be raped in my lifetime.

Life changed and took a turn after that. I was just a shell of a teenager living in a home with no emotional support, no one to turn to, nowhere to go, and not a clue what I was doing with my life.

By fifteen and a half, I wasn't going to school, I wasn't really serving any good or useful purpose for anyone, and the boy I was dating his family was moving to Las Vegas and asked if perhaps I would want to go.

So I shared the story with my (step)mom. I figured she wouldn't care as she wasn't emotionally or physically invested in me or my well-being and she agreed to let me go encouraged me. She was always quick to encourage me dating even at a very young age, however also quick to call me a slut or a whore for doing so. There was no pleasing her.

I t wasn't long after moving to Las Vegas that I realized this was yet just another terrible turn in my life that I would have to endure and try and get out the other side of.

Was there something wrong with me? Was I cursed? Why did nothing ever go right?

M y boyfriend's parents were both alcoholics and it appeared they had an issue with gambling as well, so our days were filled with going to the local union meetings to see if we could find work to buy food and maybe pay our way but most days, work was not what we got.

. . .

I learned very early on and quickly that a girl with, let's just say, decent looks, could just ask for things.

I also learned that in Las Vegas people were very fast to offer you a drink but no one ever asked if you wanted a sandwich or something to eat.

Things between the boyfriend and I got worse very quickly as there was no work, no money, and no way to contribute, so again I serve no good or useful purpose.

The worse it got the more physically aggressive things got and at one point during an argument he kicked me down a concrete set of stairs. I never got medical attention but years later found out I had fractured my tailbone, and to this day cannot have pressure at base of tailbone.

S hould be easy to say that that was the end of that. Now what I had to do was figure out how I was going to get back home or I should say to California or anywhere else other than Las Vegas

I was emaciated, drained, and defeated, so I called home crying and desperate which resulted in being picked up and taken back to California.

Now I'm back in California with no self-esteem, living with my stepmom who was not at all happy to have me. So I of course resort to the only thing I know: which is seeking love and attention in all the wrong places.

I started spending time with a young lady who like myself enjoyed the party and back then in the 70s it was not all too hard to have a fake ID and get into clubs where you could drink and get in nothing but trouble.

One of these such outings we ended at a small club in downtown Riverside that was below the old courthouse.

We got in and of course one after the other drinks were bought for us by the plethora of men that frequented this particular establishment. During this one particular night a gentleman was paying especially close attention to me, buying my drinks and staying very near.

I noticed that I didn't feel right, then I became dizzy and slightly incoherent. The last thing I remember is him "taking me outside to get some air."

My memories are foggy after that. I can remember going in and out of consciousness. I remember there being more than one man in the room and then finally becoming "awake" for lack of a better term. I was held down and three men took turns raping me, this went on for hours until dawn.

The next morning I found myself partially dressed, very sore and being escorted to a car where two men drove me back to the general area from which I came and dropped me off on the side of the road. Just like a bag of garbage. And that's exactly what I felt like.

You can surmise this didn't do much for my self-esteem, and to be quite frank back in those days it wasn't discussed much, but now, at my age with 22 years of experience in the mental health field, I can tell you I was clinically depressed.

I am sure some of you are saying, "Get it together", figure life out, get help, etc…That is so much easier said than done. I had no idea HOW to get help!!!

I proceeded to do the wrong things, to get in trouble. I didn't go to school, didn't have an education, didn't have a job, didn't have direction, didn't have guidance, didn't have a life really.

I was 17 years old and had already lived a lifetime of abuse, neglect and trauma. What was the point to all that? Why was I even alive…

.  .  .

As life went on I continued to drink too much and as a result ended up being kicked out once again from my stepmother's house and was temporarily staying with my brother who had a small condo near the university he attended.

Not too long after this living arrangement started trouble found me again under the influence when police pulled my girlfriend and I over (not in a vehicle.)

And gave us a sobriety test and then took us into the station this resulted in my stepmother being contacted. She refused to be involved at all and referred my custody to my biological father which resulted in contacting my biological mother, who lived at the time in the state of Colorado. I had not seen or spent time with her since I was a child. I could not imagine that change and I begged and pleaded promising to be better. No one cared.

Fast forward and suddenly I'm on a plane flying to Colorado not knowing what to expect when moving in with my biological mother, her now-husband and her two small sons in a single wide, two bedroom trailer. It was a shock for all. SO uncomfortable and awkward.

Well no surprise that didn't last long either. Probably three months into it, after I had actually gotten myself into college ( I took my GED and passed in 2/12 hrs) and found a job, My mother told me that her husband no longer could tolerate my sleeping on the couch and that he wanted me out. I had become an unwelcome guest and reminder of a past he just as soon forget.

So my biological mother, who at the time cleaned houses for a living, drove me to one of her client's homes, took me inside with the only suitcase I had with my clothes, and led me to a room. She told me I'd be living there now. The homeowner was elderly, kind and had a dog. I thought , ok I've certainly had worse.

Now I'm 18 and at some point, all the person has are their instincts, so I continued to work, purchased a vehicle (please remember this is the 70 so it was only a few hundred dollars), and proceeded to live my life on a day-to-day basis.

I met a boy, I suppose you could say a man-boy as he was an adult and I was now eighteen. He worked as a mechanic and I worked the swing shift at a factory.

He was wild but seemed nice. Rode a Harley Davidson in the summer and drove a truck in the winter. He treated me fine. Nothing special of course, I was so absorbing of ANY attention I would not have been able to recognize healthy love so would not have known the difference between good, bad, or indifferent at that point in my life.

After a couple of months of dating he asked if I wanted to move in with him. By then we were spending most of our time together and I certainly wasn't all that comfortable living with a complete stranger. It seemed the safer way to go again, not that I knew the difference between the two.

So I moved in with him. Everything was fine for a while. We drank a lot. Back in those days it seems everybody drank too much, too often, and he also smoked a lot of marijuana. And of course, the 70s were filled full of all kinds of other fun chemicals as well mushrooms, cocaine and you name it.

After about six months of living together things started to change. I started seeing a side of him that I hadn't seen before, which was that of anger and then after fists of anger a complete disconnection. He would drink or smoke himself into oblivion. To say we had a lack of communication is a severe understatement.

Well as I am sure you would all expect that is the end of this chapter.

One day boy gets mad, hits girl, and while man-boy's at work girl calls brother in California, emotionally distressed, and hatches a plan. She sells everything she can find that's not nailed down, buys herself a plane ticket, and leaves Colorado.

So back to Riverside, California I go!!!!

3

---

# YOU ARE AN ADULT NOW, RIGHT??

OK well things have changed, since now I'm eighteen years old. That means I'm an adult right?

That couldn't be further from the truth.

Anyway, once I return, I move in with my brother and his then-fiancé and life goes on moving forward. Bigger and better they say.

Here's the problem I'm eighteen. I'm lost. I'm confused. I'm traumatized. I'm abused. I'm uneducated and struggle with no direction and no means to take care of myself.

This doesn't last long in a young person's life. My brother and his fiancée were 22. They're trying to live their lives and having me sleeping on the couch proved to be a problem. I was always a nuisance, in the way, not belonging..Why am I here, why am I alive?

We had some discussions and arrangements were made, but after not too long I'm bouncing around in the streets trying to work, trying to survive, trying to eat, trying to live.

Eventually, I would end up back with my stepmother in Riverside, trying to get a fresh start. Try not to laugh out loud, I know it's a sad joke.!!

. . .

I'm sure a fresh start for most people is certainly different than a fresh start for me.

Tension in the house at this point was much higher than it had ever been before.

I'm guessing because I was an actual adult and the expectation was high as far as what I should be doing and how I should be doing it. Even though no one had ever given me the tools or guidance to become an adult or what those expectations would be.

And so I would fail miserably.

The one thing I always seem to have as my skill set, was my ability to attract men. I think about it now and wonder if I had a particular scent? Could they smell the desperation, the neediness, abuse and victim disposition on me?

I never lacked for male attention, and although it wasn't necessarily what I wanted it was something I learned I could use to my advantage and so I did.

Well this year, 1981, brought many wonderful things into my life and also brought many not so wonderful things as well. No big surprise there.

I met a young musician, but he was more of a producer. He had been a performer and this took me on a journey into my untapped talent of music on a level that I had not yet experienced. I had been professionally in the music industry since a teen, mostly doing commercials and music for soundtracks but nothing all that spectacular since I was very young. (one of the highlights of my younger life)

But that was about to change.

I started working on demos now. I even started getting hired to do backup vocals for musicians and artists that were on the radio and it was so terribly exciting.

Unfortunately I still had a lot of demons.

I still had no idea what I was doing. I still had no self-esteem and was incredibly insecure, so I was an easy target and easy to take advantage of.

Simultaneously a lot of things were happening. I've got this great part of my life where I can find solace and some peace in my music and sharing that with others. But the other side is never knowing what's happening, why it's happening, and consequently always finding myself in a bad situation, dangerous surroundings and trouble lurking not far away.

Let's keep in mind that this is 1981 which means it's a revolution of drugs and alcohol, sex and rock 'n' roll . All of those things combined and I was certainly smack dab in the middle of it.

All of this and guess what? I meet a man and I mean a man. He is 34 years old, he has a son, and he seems interested in me. I am 19

Now mind you I'm basically living in a minefield. My home life is tense and chaotic. There's no love, no guidance, no security. Most of the time I just felt like a nuisance and of course as if I didn't belong. My step mother had no patience for me and most days I felt as if she would rather me be dead

A short snippet on a moment when I was asked out on a date by this 34-year-old man.

. . .

I have very little clothing as I had come back with hardly anything at all and of course no job or any money to buy anything. I was too proud, probably too embarrassed; to ask anyone else, like a friend, to borrow something to wear so I had a red with white polka dot sundress that I thought would be nice. Unfortunately, the only shoes I had to my name were a pair of black flip flops, so I asked my stepmother if I could borrow a pair of shoes to wear on my date.

Of course the answer was no. It seemed she went out of her way to cause me pain, maybe because I was my father's daughter or just because she really hated me.

I suppose it didn't matter after all, this thirty-four-year-old man might just be flattered that a nineteen-year-old would accept a date from him or was just another man wanting to exploit me. Either way we enjoyed our date and each other's company and that date led to a very fast and intimate relationship.

So before you know it rather than living with my stepmother in a very uncomfortable and unloving environment I moved in with a 34-year-old and began a very short-lived relationship with him.

Good news is no more living with stepmom and perpetuating the trauma inflicted on me since I was a small child.

It's still 1981. Lots of drugs, alcohol, and other shenanigans. So imagine being nineteen and living with a thirty-four-year-old would come with its perks: alcohol in the house, access to a vehicle, and, of course, money.

Now just in case you are wondering, it should go without saying that I'm as responsible with money as a five-year-old in the candy store. I've never been taught responsibility, how to balance a checkbook, how to be budget conscious, or anything for that matter.

So during this short-lived relationship I spent time with

people my age or age group while he worked I decided to go to dental school to become a dental assistant.

But this too was very short-lived. I was much too drawn to the life of partying and now I had money and a car and a way to indulge and indulge is what I did.

21

The relationship ultimately ended pretty quickly with he and I breaking up but not before he asked me what I wanted for my birthday and my response was for him sign over the pink slip to his car on my 20<sup>th</sup> birthday , and he did. I still feel shame and remorse for taking advantage of that situation, but I didn't know I was taking advantage, I only knew how to survive.

I was hopeful my twenties could and would teach me some much needed life skills, let's see how that goes.!!!

# 4

# THE ROARING 20S, OR IS IT ROLLING?!?

So here I am freshly out of another dysfunctional relationship, still clearly suffering from my reactive attachment disorder and even more my post-traumatic stress disorder from all of the trauma in my life up until this point.

Not many days go by now without me thinking about how I've lived a life of neglect, how my parents had basically disowned me if they ever owned me to begin with.

How being molested from the age of three until fourteen, had damaged my ability to gauge relationships and recognize love or affection from someone in a way that was sincere and healthy.

These days were filled with pain and depression and hopelessness this lead to my belief that drinking or doing drugs or anything else was better than drowning in these thoughts and memories.

So my priority was having fun and finding love, obviously not even knowing what that meant or looked like, as no one had ever showed me healthy love or did anything to ever protect me. Instead, they just took it advantage of me, hurt me, and used me. And those models of life were replicated by me, as I know I hurt and took advantage of others as well.

. . .

I'd venture off, spending most of my days drinking or getting high to no real purpose and by now dental school has completely become a thing of the past.

Thank goodness for a cheerful personality and pleasant appearance. It was never difficult for me to get a job or find a way to make money, now as an adult woman.

I was still doing the music thing as often as I could and did waitressing, which back then was instant money, which meant instant gratification.

Even for lack of guidance in teaching and parenting, I still seemed to always manage to figure just enough out to keep going. My survival mode, eat or be eaten.

So days turned into weeks and weeks into months. Mostly just surviving. Wanting so much more for myself but not having a clue about how to get it and entering into one bad relationship after the other.

For those that don't know it, through counseling I learned that when you are sexually abused at a young age you equate love to sex, so you're looking for a suitor or a man to call your own and you use your sexuality to draw them in and count on that just to stay in the

Now the disclosure...That never works. Love really has nothing to do with sex. Shocker!!

Of course, a sexual relationship is important to loving your partner, but I've since learned that intimacy is much more than a physical act.

So around twenty-four, I met a guy like most others, he seemed nice and that he cared about me and my well-being.

He came from a family of money so they were certain expectations.

And I was not a prize pick for this mama's boy.

I honestly feel that he cared about me. However, I wouldn't really know what that looks like still and so I, as always, blind fully and optimistically thought , "this is the one".

His family, however, made it very difficult as they didn't approve of me and felt I was beneath them.

As if I needed one more person to tell me I was worth nothing. I already questioned my existence and what seemed my only purpose was to find someone who was able to help me understand that I did deserve to be alive and that I did have purpose.

I'm sure a lot of people are probably thinking, "Gee how did you ever have the strength to keep going or not want to kill yourself?"

Let's us not be confused: killing myself was a thought I had more often than not during my 20s and again in my late 40s and early 50s.

At the same time, I think I've always had this strange feeling that something bigger than me had me here for a purpose. That I was meant to be here, and that if somehow I just held onto the goodness that I felt inside then I could share that with someone else and it would help. The promise of more, of a happy life.

Anyway, back to the story.

So I recall the first Thanksgiving when he and I were to spend it with his family at a beautiful home they had in Lake Arrowhead, California.

We drove up and many family members were there. Everyone of course was kind and interacting with one another but very cold and distant to me.

When it came time to sit down for dinner, his mother had very meticulously placed everyone at the table and coincidentally enough, there was neither a table setting nor a chair for me to sit.

Standing there was excruciatingly embarrassing, and no one said a word. No one did anything. They went on about their meal and what they were doing without even the slightest care. I fled from the room and I remember going outside at some point.

There was a hot tub on the patio and I sat there with what I think it was wine, crying and wondering why it was happening to me.

At these times of weakness and vulnerability I ask myself *why* a lot. Why me? Why again? Why every time? Why can't it be better? Why doesn't anyone love me? Why didn't my parents love me.... it was a conversation I'd had with myself more times than I could count.

The time passed quickly that day after that (and one of the things I realized and I might've mentioned when I was living in Vegas), is that it's always fairly easy to get your hands on alcohol but being offered food or a place to stay is a completely different story.

The alcohol was easily accessible and I certainly proceeded to have my share. So much so that I became highly inebriated, which brought out my sadness that very quickly turned into frustration and escalated to anger.

I'm sure you can guess what happens next and that I completely embarrassed myself and my boyfriend and seemed to prove the point to his mother that I was definitely not good enough.

I suppose I felt "lucky for me" that he didn't dump me right away.

We moved into an apartment close to the college where he was attending. And because I wasn't working full-time, I thought it might not be a bad idea for me to go back to school as well and I did.

The longer we were together the more angry and frustrated and unhappy he and I both became.

He was verbally abusive and physically abusive, but at this point in life I was used to that. Everyone had been that way toward me, so I almost always expected it.

I remember at such a young age, thirteen maybe fourteen, my stepmother always telling me what a whore I was and how useless I was and how I would never amount to anything.

Now, you're probably also thinking "Where in the world is this girl's father?" they say the relationship between a father and his daughter is a very important one. It shapes and helps a girl understand how she should be treated by a man.

Well if that's the case then you should know that the last memories I have of my father are that of him hitting me upside my left shoulder, neck and head with a 2 x 4. Then about four years later when I rushed to his bedside while he lay dying in the hospital from a torn aorta, I grabbed his hand with tears in my eyes and he took his hand away and looked my brother in his face and asked "Why is she here?"

I can't remember now if I mentioned much about the very strange relationship I had with my biological father. I will just add that since the date of my conception, after my birth, and my entire life, he never accepted me as his own and very often publicly stated that he did not believe I was of his blood.

He was not a good man, aside from the obvious things, including his involvement in organized crime.

He was angry and had a deep hatred for women.

It showed in every action, in every relationship he ever had, up until his dying day while I look down on him and he continued to disown me...

Seems life kept continuing to show me that perhaps both my father and my stepmother were right...

B ack to the boyfriend.
As time went on the abuse escalated. It became more physical and more painful and he started to introduce strange and painful sexual requirements into the relationship.

At one point, a friend of his brought over a small battery

with cords attached and clamps that at the time I didn't know but would be used for nipples.

You guessed it, Mine!!!!

So over 3 years in and more abuse than I can possibly share: emotional, mental, physical, sexual. It was getting to the point where I wasn't sure I could take much more. Of course those thoughts of just ending my life and making it easier for everyone crossed my mind constantly.

All the while, I'm still working on an achievement: getting my degree in business and psychology, however not even knowing what I would do with it at the time.

I was such a shell of a person. No confidence, no direction, no understanding of life, and how it could or should be.

Just what you saw on television or at the movies. Even so broken, I dreamed of a fairytale ending. A knight in shining armor on his white horse.

I was in contact with a girlfriend that I had met when I was nineteen. She had actually dated the producer that I was working with back then and we had kept in contact over the years.

She was a beautiful blonde with a bubbly personality and was living in my hometown.

I shared with her what I was going through. Of course, she was shocked and mortified and told me I had to get out, but I had nowhere to go. I had no money saved. All I really had was a $300 car that barely ran and still somehow a will to live and have something better.

So one day, I packed my clothes and what a few personal items I had in my beat up little car and drove back to Riverside, California and moved in with my girlfriend and her then-boyfriend. I had no more life skills and understanding then before this chapter.

Oddly enough I felt more compassion and had a stronger

desire to find love and happiness. The more pain I endured the more I thrived to be happy.

It wasn't long before I was deep into what they were, that popular pastime of partaking in the use of methamphetamines. I had no idea what I was getting in to. I had never seen this side of drug use. The shady and seedy side.

This was definitely a turn for the worse.

Because of my drug use, it became so much more difficult to work consistently and make money, or for that matter even make good choices with what to do with my life. I'm twenty seven, still with no direction, no guidance, no love, no support, and killing brain cells by the minute.

However Tamera being Tamera and doing what she knew best, I was surviving.

Trying to stay on the grind and always making sure that she had someone's attention.

Or, more specifically, a man's attention, which always provided me with occasional meals, nights out, sleepovers, and sometimes gifts.

There were many of these types over the course of the next two years and there was also a lot of drug use, alcohol, and promiscuous sex.

One of said encounters ended in me contracting an STD.

I'm sure it will sound funny to say that I'm grateful it was only gonorrhea, and was curable by an antibiotic.

But I was then and am now forever grateful that it wasn't something worse, sex is and never will be worth dying for.

I suppose if I'm being completely candid and honest now I need to share that during these times, dating all the way back to the boy in Colorado, I almost never used protection or birth control. There were unwanted pregnancies in addition to all the other consequences I faced during these years.

My first was a very traumatizing and horrific experience because the boy paying for it didn't want to pay extra for anesthesia. I only had a general, which means I was awake during the procedure. It is something I remember vividly to this day, the sound of the procedure and the machinery, the look on the nurse's faces especially the one holding my hand, and the gut wrenching pain both physically and mentally knowing and understanding that I was ending the life of what would have been my child.

**B**ack to the storyline
I meet what seems to be a decent guy. He worked for car dealership, had a good family. He had also been married and had two small children. I mean how much more normal can you get right?

My drug use is not excessive, nor had ever really been other then varied "binging" moments.

The problem was and always would be that it wasn't about how normal the other person was but how incredibly not normal I was.

**I** was a traumatized child inside a woman's body, never knowing if any decision I made was the right one and living my life purely on instinct and survival.

So Mr. Normal is a great guy. He takes me out to dinner, he buys me gifts, he treats me like a real woman. I don't think he sees that petrified child inside begging for love and acceptance just the pretty package it's wrapped up in.

So about six or seven months into dating, I become pregnant.

I'm paralyzed with fear not only to tell him but what his response might be and of course having clear vivid memory of what it was like to be in this position previously.

But I kept thinking this guy is different. He's normal. Remember, he has a great family, he already has kids so he likes kids. He'll probably ask me to marry him and you'll have a baby of your own to love and take care of.

Well, I hope whoever is reading this isn't too terribly

surprised or disappointed to hear that his response was not a marriage proposal.

He actually said that his mother wanted to sit down with the three of us so that we could discuss the "situation."

The way he said it made it so obviously clear that it wasn't going to be a conversation that had a happy ending, at least not for me.

So within a twenty-four hour period, there I sat in the living room at his mother's home—a wonderful woman, a great grandmother, a businesswoman successful in her career. I think today we would call her a "Boss."

She kindly started to talk about how her son had already been married, and had two children, and how difficult it was for him and her family under those circumstances, and that she thought I was a lovely girl, and that she was sorry that we hadn't been more responsible and made better choices allowing this to happen.

She then advised that she thought it was best for everybody that the pregnancy be terminated. But presented to me, as if a bonus prize, a full-time job at her company, so that once I have physically recovered I could go to work and start my life over.

A life that didn't include her son.

I don't think that during this entire conversation I was ever really given any choice. However, as a woman we always have a choice, but my paralyzing fear overcame me once again, and the idea of having a baby and being single while not having money, going on welfare and not having anywhere to live, petrified me so I accepted her offer as kindness and allowed her to pay for the termination of the pregnancy with a job waiting for me upon my recovery.

After the procedure, a girlfriend was kind enough to let me convalesce in her home.

I was feeling of course lost and unloved, but had a glimmer of hope that I managed to always hold onto and that I would have a job soon and a way to take care of myself.

While on the mend what should happen? I met another man.

He was not my type, at all.

Tall, skinny, long hair, and acne.

But oddly enough, it was easy to see past all of that and that he had a good heart and a sharp sense of humor. I was more broken than I had ever been before, it was all too much for me.

His conversations were a welcome event. I am not sure life would have gone on for me much longer under my current circumstances.

I was very honest with him from the start and told him why I was there and what I was going through. He was always kind and listened even though a little sarcastic.

He would come over almost every day after work just to hang out and talk and I always looked at him as just a friend. After a few months of kindness, support and encourage the way I looked at him changed. I thought, clearly I have NOT made good choices in men. Usually being attracted to muscular, athletic types this man was the complete opposite. Hey maybe that's exactly what I needed. The unfamiliar, the different, the unlikely…And kindness went a long way for me, even though my nativity never really allowed me to make good choices

As soon as I was able to get up and around it was time to go to work.

I had my little beater car to get me there and back but I was certainly concerned as it very quickly did not like the drive from Fontana to Ontario and started having mechanical issues.

So out of nowhere this new friend, a sarcastic, funny man offered to allow me to use his truck to go to work and back as he had a partner that would be able to drive him.

It was one of the kindest things anyone had done for me for a very long time and I was gracious and humbled in accepting his offer.

Now of course, because I was driving his truck every day, it meant that we would see each other every night when he would come to pick up the vehicle.

It started that just staying for a little while would turn into staying overnight. We would talk into the wee hours of the morning before getting a little sleep and sharing stories of our lives.

He listened to everything I told him. Everything about myself, my childhood, my terrible choices in men, the friendships that had broken me, and the family I didn't have.

I would cry when I talked about how I lived a life so unloved and how the recent termination of my pregnancy only made all of that so much more real.

I had no one and nothing to my name but my own few personal belongings.

No home, no family!!

So as the days turned into weeks and then months we spent almost every evening together, we started having conversations about who we were, who we were together, and what we wanted out of life and from each other.

He talked about family and how he always wanted kids because he never really had that growing up. He had recently found out that he was adopted and there was so much hurt and anger behind living thirty-six years always knowing that he didn't fit in but never being given the honesty of where he came from so that he could identify with who he was.

His adoptive parents were older and raised him differently than other kids his age.

He was overprotected and stifled, but most importantly he was lied to, and that had broken something inside of him.

So after a few months of all of these deep conversations, and time spent together, a friendship grew into a deep love and understanding of one another.

His desire to have family and a wife and a future was all music to my ears.

But there were red flags.

He drank too much, he did drugs, and I sensed that he had a deep anger.

But, as usual, I ignored those red flags and listened to the sweet words of how I would be loved, and taken care of, and have a home and a family and a future.

And I was *ALL* in.

We got an apartment and we were both still working when I found out I was pregnant.

I know you think I would have learned at this point and at this age. I'm now 29 and I should be more careful and think things through.

But I'd never been given those tools. I'd never been taught or shown how to make the right decision. My life has always been living on a wing and a prayer. I wish I could change that about my past but how could I have?

This time it seemed it was different there was excitement and anticipation. What I thought was love and a future to look forward to. Normal, as if I knew what that was, but darn it I was gonna fake it till I made it.

And when I saw how excited he was, and I knew how I felt about it, there was a sense of calm and a sense of knowing. A very unfamiliar state of mind

I believed I would finally have what I had always dreamed of.

A family.

A baby to love and nurture.

A man who would love me and support me and our baby and take care of everything.

As a beautiful being grew inside of me, I was overjoyed with all of the things that came with being pregnant.

I would sit for hours with a Walkman headset on my stomach playing Mozart, Beethoven or Dr. Seuss.

I would talk to my baby and tell it how amazing of a life it was going to have and I would love it more than any mother had ever loved a child.

At approximately five months pregnant we got married. It was at his parents church, my biological father even gave me away, (even though he had offered money for the groom to run away).

My brother was there and all of our friends.

It felt surreal.

Normal, for lack of a better term almost like I was a regular person and that I had this regular life.

A normal life like everyone else like the families that you see on TV or the ones you read about in books, or saw in your neighborhood growing up.

It was a good day. Not a great day but a good day. But there were drugs involved, arguments and a sense of darkness over everything.

But I pushed the thought away that I was probably just being paranoid about life and that a never-ending wait for the other shoe to drop or something terrible to happen was status quo, because that's my life as I knew it.

But nothing happened that day or for any other day for the next five months.

My baby girl was swimming around in utero for over ten months.

And I felt like I was the happiest pregnant woman on the planet even though I looked like the side of a full moon.

I remember I made T-shirts that said "I'm not fat I'm pregnant" from the .99 Cents store and acrylic fabric paint.

I must've worn those almost every day the last two months of my pregnancy.

I was deliriously happy, and could not wait to meet the person I knew I would love more than I had ever loved anything or anyone before.

And after almost ten and a half months the doctor said I think we should go in and take this baby or it's going to stay there forever.

We laughed and scheduled the C-section for three days later.

On February 22 at 9:35 AM my little girl was brought into this world.

I had a spinal block so I couldn't feel anything, and they had me papered off from my abdomen as they have to cut you from side to side and remove your organs laying them on your chest to remove the baby.

But I heard her cry and I started to cry, her daddy went with the nurse to clean her and measure her and give her Apgar score, which was a nine although to ask her father he would always sat she was a ten for sure.

They brought her to me and laid her on my chest.

And even now I cannot put into words what it was that I felt.

My heart was so full.

And I felt the most calm and at peace I think I ever had.
This was it, this was the beginning of life.
A life I had never known. A love like I'd never felt.
In the hope of a future I had never seen.
This child was my everything.
The one thing I had done right in my entire life, up until this point.
My reason for existence.
My destiny.
The perfect ending right?
Nothing is ever that easy!!!
At least not for me...

# 5

# BABY MAKES THREE, THEN THERE'S JUST ME

Having this precious little girl was so life-changing. I've never felt so happy, so elated, so overjoyed.

I was beaming with happiness.

Everything in life made sense. It was euphoric having this little human that depended on me for absolutely everything.

I so quickly became a completely different person.

I had been a person who couldn't seem to make a good decision. Who didn't have a clue how to take care of themselves or plan a future or balance a checkbook.

I was a mother now.

And with that came huge responsibility and I embraced it as if I had been doing it all my life.

This was clearly the most magical time of my life. I had this beautiful baby that brought me a type of joy I had never felt.

I was so in love and so fiercely protective of this amazing little life that I was gifted with.

I can't believe that which should be one of the happiest times of my life could turn into just another life experience that would leave me broken and changed forever.

.   .   .

I think I need to backtrack just a little at this time to share some information. It's not going to shine a good light on me but is important to the story because so many choices were made and so many things happened and I am certainly responsible for many of them.

So with that said I should share. While I was pregnant during my short courtship with my then husband, having already mentioned that he had an addiction to methamphetamine and alcohol, I was party to illegal actions that allowed him to use his drugs freely without taking money out of the pocket of his family.

In layman's terms, I was dealing drugs.

I was the pick-up person and I would pick up large quantities of methamphetamine bring them home and distribute them for sale.

This is not something I'm proud of, but of course in my mind at the time I reasoned away the fact that it was not only illegal and immoral, in addition to dangerous, but that financially it was the right thing to do for my family.

So this is what I did throughout my pregnancy. We made a good deal of money and we secured a home, vehicles, and extra items, and when the day came for my daughter's arrival, I felt very prepared and bringing her home and us being safe.

I had discussed with my husband how what we were doing could not be continued. The risks that had been taken up to that point were many and the one thing I wasn't willing to risk was the safety of my child.

As I mentioned, my pregnancy lasted over ten months. I was much overdue, and based on what the doctors told me my daughter had no intention of coming out on her own. So we scheduled a C-section at 9:30 on a Friday and prep to go to the hospital.

. . .

Like almost everything else in my life it was a complicated birth. I couldn't take the epidural, due to bone spurs, so they ended up having to give me a spinal block which meant I was basically numb from the neck down.

All I remember is the doctor and all of the nurses saying "Oh my God" and of course that freaked me out, thinking that karma had caught up to me and was going to punish me for my bad deeds.

As it turns out, the gasps were all about this newborn who had a full head of hair and weighed almost eleven pounds and looked more like a six month-old baby than a newborn.

I, like most mothers, can never put into words what it feels like to see this little human that's been cooking inside of you finally emerge and breathe air on their own.

Their cute little fingers and toes and chubby little cheeks.

My heart melted and also became that of a lion at the same moment.

For me, maternal instincts were natural.

All I wanted to do was love, protect, and provide for this beautiful little girl and there wasn't anything or anyone that would be able to stop me from doing that.

After two days in the hospital it was time to go home.

I was so focused and busy with my new responsibilities as a mother that I really didn't pay attention or notice much else that was going on around me at least for the first few months.

But if I'm being honest, whatever relationship had ever really existed between my husband and I was already fading, as it became so clear so quickly that not only our parenting styles but our priorities were nothing in the same.

He was not a hands-on father. He never fed her or changed her diapers ,cleaned up after her, or even held her much for that matter.

I don't doubt that he loved her in the only way that he knew how, but perhaps he was afraid, because she was so small and he was going to be responsible for this little human being and he could barely take care of himself.

He continued to drink and do drugs on a daily basis.

And obviously me watching this while being the responsible parent for the child just made the relationship deteriorate that much more quickly.

A few months after bringing her home from the hospital my husband got in a work related accident and tested positive for drugs.

He was put on probation and asked to enter a rehabilitation program.

He reluctantly went to the program, but he never really invested in recovery, as he never had any intention of ever changing his lifestyle. I don't think he believed he was doing anything wrong.

Obviously this would have an effect on our relationship as well, in addition to the fact that as I stated he never really spent time with our daughter. There was no bonding there and it was heartbreaking to watch.

After completing his 30-day program he went back to work and it wasn't 60 days later he was busted again on the job testing positive for drugs.

This time he was terminated.

Now, life is thrown into a panic. What do we do? How do we pay the mortgage? How do we buy food? And who's going to help take care of my baby.

I refused to have drugs in the house, but because he wasn't working he said that was the only way he could create an income.

I got to the point to where I couldn't sleep. I figured that the police would knock the door down and find drugs in the house and take my baby away.

I told him I'd go back to work but that he would have to make sure her needs were met and that she had to have a diaper changed and bathed and fed and all of the other things that come along with being responsible for a child. I don't know how

I could've trusted that he would do the right thing and be a good parent, it was a very stressful time.

I'm sure you can only imagine how nerve-racking this was for me, the idea leaving my child alone with her father was not the question. It was who he was as a father. The alcohol, the drugs, the irresponsible lifestyle. I was a mess with nerves and anxiety.

On my fourth day of employment, I was overwhelmed with the feeling of dread and I wasn't handling how that made my anxiety rise and I asked my boss if I could make a phone call or even drive home quickly to check on my baby and he said that if I left I would lose my job.

I couldn't fight the feeling. I just knew instinctively that there was something wrong, so I walked to my car and I drove home and when I open the door I was horrified.

It was probably 2 o'clock in the afternoon and the house was filled with marijuana smoke. There was white powder on the coffee table and beer cans everywhere. In the midst of it all, there was a child not even nine months old with just a diaper on, Cheetos orange dust on her fingers and face, and bodies and faces of people that I've never met or seen before.

Well, if you guessed correctly then you know I blew a gasket. I mean I lost my shit.

Screaming and yelling and at that point. All I knew was that the only important thing in the world was this poor vulnerable child who didn't asked to be brought into this world, but needed my protection and my love and my care.

I kicked everyone out including my husband and told him that was it. No more. I could take no more.

I changed the locks and basically never looked back from there.


My only focus was taking care of my beautiful little girl, the love of my life, the one gift that I have been given in my 30 years that I cherished. I was going to do anything and everything I had to in order to raise her and give her a life that she deserved.

That was no easy task.

My ex-husband stalked me over the course of five years. He got me fired from every job I had.

He would drag me in and out of court, almost every other month, because he wanted something other than supervised visitation.

The court order required me to drive my daughter to his house every other weekend and allow him to be supervised by his parents who he lived with.

Unfortunately, his parents were huge enabler's and over the years many issues arose. One of the more severe ones was when my little girl was about five, I got a call from the emergency room. While under the influence, he had wrapped his car around a light post. By the time I got to the hospital, my little girl was lying in a hospital bed on a traction board, her body bruised from neck to thigh.

I'm not sure how I maintained myself the way I did, not breaking down crying, not screaming, even though inside I just wanted to put my hands around his throat.

But what mattered most was that little girl, so beautiful with that blonde hair and sky blue eyes looking at me trusting me.

Once again, I just said, I gotta do everything and anything I can to keep her safe and healthy and as happy as possible, as much as I hated driving her to the house and leaving her with somebody so incapable and selfish.

That was her biological father, and having lived the life I had, I didn't have the heart to break hers.

If only she had known what I had gone through over the course of those last five years. The middle of the night visits from strangers who would hold a gun to my head and tell me that I needed to let her father have better visitation or the next time they visited I might be left not standing.

The financial struggles that I had to go through because he got me fired from almost every job.

Raising a child without the financial means to provide for them was very difficult especially since I never received child support. My ex-husband never went back to work after being terminated for drug use.

I honestly don't know what his hustle was or how he made money. I never spoke to him on any real level after we separated.

What he had that we didn't was a home. He had a roof over his head and the security of his parents providing for him, even though at this point he was over 40 years old.

They rarely bought anything for my beautiful little girl—no diapers, no baby wipes, no clothes.

It truly was a struggle for many, many years. But the love and happiness of that beautiful smiling face gave me hope and strength always.


When she turned six, I met a man at my place of employment. And I was turning 36, I was working for the phone company and that was probably one of the biggest corporations I had worked for and I was excited at the prospect of a great career and meeting new and profession peers.

He and I bonded over children and it was obvious to me, very early on, that he was a bit old-fashioned.

He was eight years older than I was, and had previously been married for sixteen years.

And honestly, what I saw in him was something I'd never seen before or for that matter ever experienced, and that was stability, or so I thought.

The idea of having that stable home life, a husband that goes to work, steadily bringing in a paycheck, contributing to the home, mowing the yard, all the things that you feel are Normal...there's that word again!!

A life I had never lived neither as a child or an adult.

. . .

We went on our first date on my birthday. There was never any real passion between us—that wasn't the kind of relationship it was—but more of kindred spirits both lonely and wanting for that normal stable family life.

We moved in rather quickly together and, as the old saying goes, had I known then what I know now, hindsight being 20/20, I would've realized it was a big mistake.

His divorce was not yet final, and by bringing me into the picture it complicated things. His ex decided to go for the throat and she had a good lawyer that knew exactly how to do that.

By the end of it all he lost 3/4 of his salary.

And I had three teenage boys coming to my house every other weekend.

The alternating weekends when there were no kids in the house could be fun. We had great friends and we liked to have fun listening to music, playing games, enjoying the swimming pool, and basking in the sun.

It could have been much worse, that is for sure. It was comfortable like I said. Certainly not passionate but comfortable.

We didn't fight yell or scream at each other. We never really disagreed on much in the early years, but it was so clear that there was something very large missing. But being this was marriage number two I was not ready to fail at something else in life.

And the stability that it provided my daughter and I was something I craved and needed.

More so for her than myself.


My focus was always on her giving her what she wanted and needed, preparing her for life, and just doing everything I possibly could to give her a life that I've never known

But I made mistakes. I'm sure all mothers do.

. . .

Two years into the relationship, I became very ill. My body was failing me and the doctors were baffled at what was happening. I was diagnosed with so many things: lupus, fibromyalgia, and ultimately MS.

And it wouldn't be for another five years until I received my thyroid diagnosis and be put on medication that would help regulate my body and help me function normally.

During this time I was out on disability from my employer and it didn't look like I would probably make it back. I'd had a carpal tunnel surgery and was going on almost a year of disability. Worker's Compensation had filed a suit and I had already started training for something else to do.

I studied for months trying to figure out what I could do. How I could create a home-based business where I could spend more time with my daughter, without dropping her off at daycare at 6 o'clock in the morning and picking her up at 6:30 at night and only having every other weekend.

I was dying inside. I knew something had to give.

So I came across medical billing and coding. I took the course and received the certification during which time my Worker's Comp suit was settled and I was given a cash settlement. I utilized the new certification, the already existing education and the settlement to initiate a fresh start, a new start , a new beginning.

We opted to purchase a home and establish roots.

After which I started the job search, within two weeks of sending out resumes I landed a job at a psychologist office.

Little did I know that that job would take me on the most wonderful and fulfilling journey, one of maturity and responsibility.

I could learn to be proud of myself and hopefully show my daughter how important it was to be independent and hard-working.

So during all this time and me being in a new marriage, what happened—and I like to think of it as was more of a course of nature—is that the every other weekend wasn't as dramatic and my daughter's father seem to care less about what was going on in my life and focused more on his relationship with his little girl. One of the good side affects or my re-marrying.

That truly filled my heart. I had waited eight years for the shift and although he still couldn't be trusted and he still had an alcohol and drug problem, that wasn't her fault and as long as I could keep her safe I wasn't going to keep them apart, I had be tortured as a child during an ugly divorce, I never wanted to inflict that pain on my own child. I felt in my heart that was what was best and did all that I could to let go of the anger and negativity surrounding years of bad energy between he and I.

So life got back to "normal", so they call it.

I was working part time but making great money and my husband was working full-time and made a fair wage and at this point two of his three teenage children had become adults so the child support payments were much more affordable.

But—wait for it—of course nothing ever goes perfectly right in my life.

T he house we bought was the cutest little place, with a swimming pool and in what should've been a lovely little neighborhood on a cul-de-sac.

But it was not lovely. The neighbor girls started bullying my daughter almost right away.

Fifth grade is a tough one and we were not in the best district.

S o I put on my mommy cape and went to work once again to make sure that my daughter had the best possible chance at life and happiness. I researched and gathered information.

She qualified for a gate program which was for a higher level of intelligence, so I was able to transfer her to a school outside of our district.

Then, because of all the problems we were having, we knew it was best to sell the house and move.

And that's exactly what we did.

By this time I had put in a lot of work building my new found career skills sand I realized that the services I provided were definitely in demand and had a high level of need in my professional field.

So I took the risk and leap of faith and decided to start my own business.

This way I could work at home which is what I always wanted to do. Be there for my daughter and watch her grow and help nurture her and provide for her and keep her safe.

*(Sidenote it's 22 years later and I still have my home-based business. I have done some things right over the years).*

The next several years were really all about my daughter. She went from being a preteen to a teenager, from fifth grade through high school.

She played the cello, she was in musical theater, she was in jazz choir. She thrived and did well at all she applied herself to, always making me very proud.

I worked hard to provide her with everything she could possibly want or need.

Did I spoil her? No question the answer is yes.

There was very little real discipline or boundaries, other than my desire and need to keep her safe and close and protected.

Those all sound like wonderful things, and they are as long as you don't smother the child in the process, or confuse yourself and think that what you're doing is helping and not hindering a child's growth.

If I could do things over again, I would make sure that I allowed her to experience more things on her own. Make more of her own mistakes at a younger age, so that she'd be prepared for what that felt like when she got older.

But hindsight is 20/20 they say. Again only knowing how to learn by my mistakes.

.  .  .

I had so many plans for her. Hopes of what she may be and become in her life.

She was always a free spirit, full of energy and her own ideas, and had a lot of mannerisms and thought processes of her father which always confused me because of the little time that they spent together when she grew up.

By the time she was a young teen, she didn't have the same kind of interest in going to grandma's house every other weekend and thankfully her dad understood that, so there wasn't a lot of pressure or guilt placed on her for those decisions.

I was overprotective. She was never allowed to be alone with boys. I didn't want her going to parties or hanging out with people that did drugs and alcohol.

I inserted myself in her life in areas that I definitely regret having done.

But I had no handbook, and I certainly had no history that could've possibly shown me or taught me how to be the perfect mother.

Not that I believe there's any perfect mother.

But now that I've had time to reflect and look at my actions, I can see where my anticipating her needs and trying to be two steps of head of everything that she wanted to do say or experience, was detrimental.

The only thing I ever wanted, from the moment I heard her cry and saw her beautiful little face, was to have a bond and relationship that would last my lifetime filled full of love that could be compared to no other.

I'm sure that my loveless marriage and just the dysfunction that I was trying to make look normal, had its affects as well.

Mostly on me and my psyche, but obviously those things would affect those around me. Because my energy was always in my daughter and her life, I suppose all that negativity that I felt and all the love that I was lacking must've somehow seeped over into my ability to parent.

I know I could be sharp and probably much of the time she felt I didn't listen to her.

*That breaks my heart now, just breaks my heart, as I long to hear your voice...*

What I do know is that ,regardless of what anybody else thinks, I know how deep the love and affection that I have for my daughter is and always will be.

Everything I did, everything I worked for, every shopping spree, every house party, every vacation, every school trip she took, and everything that she always received, was because I loved her.

I know material things don't show love. Things don't buy love. You can't replace affection with material things. But my lack of positive loving experiences growing up as a child and as an adult, were very obvious to my Aleah.

I guess I just believed, at the time, that I was giving her both, but once she became an adult and shared with me how she really felt, it was clear that I was wrong and that perhaps she didn't feel all the love that I felt and had for her. I really wish there were something I could do to change that.

Life forges on and high school graduation comes.

I spent a good deal of time filling out college applications and doing a FAFSA all things I wish now I would've encouraged her to do herself.

I also should have let her decide herself if she even wanted to go to college, or what it was that she really wanted to do.

But moving forward, she got in to college and seemed happy to get on with her life, probably out from my clutches and my roof.

And before you know it, she's not around, living in a college dorm room and experiencing life all on her own.

It didn't take long after her leaving for things in my marriage to completely fall apart.

I should probably backtrack and tell you that about a year and a half before my daughter left for college, my husband had lost his job and was on unemployment. So once again I was the major breadwinner, responsible for everything and everyone. Although I always had a brave face, I don't think anyone ever knew how I was dying inside.

At this point, after a year and a half of unemployment, my husband began to drink even more heavily, in addition to taking an excessive amount of Vicoden. I would work a ten hour day in my home office and he would spend the day watching television and drinking beer.

I couldn't motivate him to save my life.

And the more unhappy he became, the more unhappy he was with me, and the more miserable my life became.


At this point, we hadn't slept in a bed together or been intimate for over eight years. I know a lot of people say *Jiminy Christmas how could you ever.*

I reiterate that my focus and my energy was always on taking care of my daughter. I wasn't going to get a divorce in the middle of her teenage years and try to figure out how to do it all over again. It was easier to stay and try to make things normal for the sake of family. I know that sounds crazy and maybe a little lazy, but what my daughter needed always came before what I needed.

With that said, by the time she left I couldn't imagine being with this man for much longer and as it turns out I wasn't.

But it wasn't until having a major mental meltdown. It was 2009, and my daughter was getting ready to start college in the fall. She really barely spent much time at home anyway, and it was summer.

My stepmother had come to visit.

I was just taxed. It took everything in me to smile and be nice and try to act normal and cook and clean and be pleasant when all I really wanted to do was scream.

And ultimately that's what ended up happening: I screamed and I yelled and I told everybody to get the hell out of my house.

That was a very big turning moment for my daughter and I don't think things were ever the same after that.

Looking back, I honestly don't know that I could've done differently. I was spinning out of control. Even though I had built a wonderful empire and a business that I could count on that created a revenue for us to live comfortably, I couldn't breathe.

I just wanted out.

I needed something. I didn't know why but I needed something. I needed to figure out my life and who I was and at this point, all I could think was *"Am I my ever going to be happy? Do I deserve happiness? Is this what life really is? Why am I even living?"*

Oh, the dark thoughts. I had plans. I would save up enough pills from my prescription refills to be able to one day just sit and take them all at one time.

Or maybe when I was driving my car and wait for an open space on the freeway and I would increase my speed and then just let go of the wheel and let the car crash into whatever was closest.

That didn't happen obviously.

Like always, I pulled myself up by my bootstraps.

Moved into a smaller more modest home. Kept working ten to twelve hour days and trying to figure out what was next.

So many things I know I'm leaving out, insofar as the life that I actually lived.

The sacrifices that I made. The life that I tried to provide for my daughter, which included trips out of the country and to at least twelve states here in the United States, all for school projects and giving her everything you possibly could material wise.

I suppose she would say that I didn't give her what she needed emotionally and if I'm totally honest she's probably right. I was so busy working and trying to give her everything I possibly could that I'd never had in my life that there were times when I probably was not emotionally available or understanding enough or listened enough. I cannot change that now, and it makes me very sad.

I just hope and pray that in the end she knows that I loved her with every fiber of my being. Perhaps not in the way that she would've wanted me to or at times needed me to but no one on this earth could possibly love her more than I did and always will!

I had basically lived the last twelve+ years of my life doing for others, putting everybody else first. Working until I thought I was capable of making sure that the bills were paid and I always had a roof over my head.

Obviously having come up the way that I did, being homeless at a very young age, having a roof and food on the table was always priority, and I would've sacrificed anything to make sure that my family had that.

Now, I am standing at this crossroad. Choosing this time to be by myself and figure out who I was and what made me happy. What I needed and what I didn't need in my life: emotionally, spiritually and physically.

It was very scary but freeing at the same time.

And as luck would have it, it was probably the best decision I've ever made as an adult, as the next several years of my journey would bring me to a place of peace and contentment and the most love I've ever felt in my entire life...

6

# IS THERE SUCH A THING AS HAPPILY EVER AFTER?

You know, for the longest time I used to say to myself things like, "Fake it till you make it" or constantly remind myself that, "This too shall pass."

But after years of self-reflection and doing a lot of hard work mentally, spiritually, and physically to find my true self, I now have a different way of speaking to myself.

Nowadays I say things like, "Happiness is an inside job" and "Today's a good day to have a good day!!!"

But I don't want to get too far ahead of myself, so let me start from the beginning of my journey.

Once out on my own and living by myself, after having to get over that ache of loneliness when you go to bed at night and wake up in the morning alone, a quiet house, no one to care for. I realized I had no clue who I was.

All I had known until then was that I was a survivor, a mother, a wife, a stepmother, a friend, and estranged daughter.

I knew it was not going to be an easy journey, but I was more prepared than I had ever been in my entire life to take it on with an open heart and an open mind.

I soon realized that words like *acceptance* and *surrender* would play a huge part in my growth and existence. And that finding myself would be the toughest and most rewarding thing I would ever do.

Now, don't get confused, this is me were talking about so nothing ever goes completely smoothly, and of course, I'm going to make mistakes.

What I missed most about myself, once I was in my own space, was being a woman.

I hadn't been kissed touched or made love to in more years than I could count. I know you're saying to yourself *but you were married.*

Yes I was, but for at least the last eight to ten years my husband and I lived under the same roof as a married couple but shared no intimacy. As a matter fact, quite the contrary, we were more like roommates than anything elsem and if I am being totally honest, we had been that way for most of the marriage.

At this point in my journey I don't choose to dwell on the negative or harbor any ill will.

It was time to forgive and move past what had ever darkened my door.

Most importantly, I had to forgive myself and release the guilt.

I recently saw a bio on a SNL cast member. He shared that throughout his therapeutic journey his therapist told him, "You must forgive yourself for the guilt you feel for having to do all the things you did to survive." That really hit me hard and felt so profound.

These type of statements are what motivated me to write this and share with the world my story, hopefully touching someone else in their own journey. In some way I hope to reach out and be a safe place of understanding for anyone who needs it.

I know what it's like to be in a dark place, I still struggle at times to know my purpose, and feel lost, and alone…wondering if my being here on this planet is even necessary or deserved.

I've always been harder on myself than anyone else ever could be, and that's saying a lot, because my whole life I've only ever wanted to be accepted, to be loved, and for someone to be proud of me and tell me I had purpose.

But that had never been the case. My bio parents gave me up, the step-family abused me, and I seemed to always choose partners that would abuse me in some way as well.

I know now that was because I was self-sabotaging and believed to my core I deserved everything I got...the hate, the anger, the abuse the pain. That was what life looked like to me. That was my "NORMAL."

I blamed myself for everything; it had to be me, right?

I could've done so many things so much differently, and things would've been so much better, had I just known more or tried harder or loved harder or listened more or thought longer or had more patience. The list goes on. I had to move forward force myself to look deeper and find the person I was who had purpose and deserved love.

I was saying, when I started this new journey, the thing I most missed about myself was being a woman. Not that I had a clear vision, because I DID NOT. I just wanted to be feminine, kind, rather than angry and depressed,, to feel worthy and appreciated. Something I had yet to feel.

B eing able to look at myself in the mirror and say, "You're beautiful." And not in a conceited kind of way, just in the way that I accepted myself for who I was, flaws and all, including the acne, freckles, cellulite, small feet, thick thighs and big butt.

I wanted to learn how to embrace myself and every part of who I was, inside and out. I started reading everything I could get my hands on with regard to loving myself. I would read everything from Rumi to Maya Angelou, Dr. Wayne Dyer to Gandhi.

I craved peace and wanted to find that place of contentment. My own personal bliss, the kind that would allow me to sleep through the night restfully and wake up the next morning feeling recharged and ready for my day happy. To be breathing and have the sight to see the beauty and wonders of our world that had been created, rather than the darkness I so often visited, where I believed that my existence was completely unnecessary.

I learned how to meditate, I did yoga, I even chanted. I fell in love with Chai Tea, created habits that would include a big cup on the back porch, meditating then maybe journaling. Who was I? I did not recognize this woman, so calm and not in a hurry. It felt better and better every passing day/week/month…

I also knew that creating new healthy habits in place of all the old ones was going to be quite an undertaking.

They say we don't break habits, you have to create new ones in their place, and that it takes a minimum of 28 days to solidify that new habit, so in saying that, every time you start, if you stop within that 28 days, you go back to day 1…It's a process, and for me one that would take quite some time.

I know it all sounds easy enough, but for me I would always find a way to sabotage…I mean it would seem like the happier I would get I'd felt guilty about being happy and question EVERYTHING I was doing and find a way to punish myself. It would end up feeling like a never ending cycle that I was unsure I could break.

But I am strong and I believed and had faith and hope, so I would get back on that path every time, determined to break the cycle and find my happy.

Everytime I fell, I got back up and tried again. I would go dark at times but I had a rule, only 48 hours in the bottom of the barrel then I had to grab my boot straps and pull myself up and try again.

Well, days turned into weeks and weeks into months and months into years, as I continued to work hard, stay healthy and forgive myself almost every day.

I reconnected with old friends and made healthy new ones that now will be there for life.

I had rituals, like gym on Tues/Thurs/Sat, different courses, weight training, cardio, zumba, yoga, depending on the day. Every Saturday morning, Chai Tea and meditation on the porch.

I actually scared myself when I could hear myself saying, "I feel great, I'm happy, I am proud of myself." As if it were someone else recognizing my accomplishments

Of course, I also had therapy. I think I will always need professional guidance, if for no other reason than to assure myself that I'm going in the right direction and I really am NOT crazy!!!

I was really growing to love and embrace time spent alone, in my thoughts and feelings. Working through all the dark stuff and letting go of the guilt and forgiving that poor little girl who did not know better.

So many things I did over the years that caused shame…I was so covered in shame that my anxiety would rise to panic at times, in public, because I was sure people could see who I was, that dirty, sad, needy, scared, stupid girl who didn't deserve to be alive because no one loved her anyway.

With time, those incidents waned, and the panic went away, and there were more times I could be proud of myself and feel worthy, as more distance was created between myself and my shame.

Life changed in so many amazing ways.

Food tasted better, and although I will always have an unhealthy relationship with food due to my PTSD, I had more respect for quality food. I stopped drinking beer and liked wine instead. The sky was bluer, the flowers were brighter, I loved the rain and change of weather, the sun felt warmer, and then I stared hearing myself say more often than not, "Life is good."

Hey wait a minute, where did that come from???? Is that true happiness? Can it stay? I want this feeling always, every day, all the time! Can I? Oh please let it stay, I need it.


Ok, so think Tamera, how to stay happy ALL the time? Well, I must be doing something right to have these feelings, yes? OK, so keep a healthy routine, push yourself outside your comfort zone, exercise and most importantly LET

GO of the guilt and shame of what was done to you and what you did to survive.

Did I have a choice? Literally I did, but did I know how to make better choices? Even after years of therapy, some trauma traits are hard to lose. However, I could see them clearer now, and I could redirect my thoughts could banish the bad much more easily. I was growing and learning and starting to thrive.

It was exciting and I wanted more. The more I wanted it the harder I worked for it. More meditation, more self-cleansing and more moments of pride and worth.

Ok, now I'm feeling like I can get out there and show the world I'm not a scared little girl, that I do deserve to live and have a life, that I am so much more than the mistakes I've made.

It's time to start living and feeling and finding out what this life and the Universe has in store for me, and deciding to be happy with whatever that is.

# 7

# FINDING THE WOMAN IN ME

I was starting, in the last chapter, to say how I had missed feeling like a woman. That soft side that attracts a "real" man. A man that is confident and appreciates a woman who works hard, but also loves being domestic.

Finding my inner woman was just another way of saying "getting in touch with my sexuality."

And a big part of that of course was intimacy.

Intimacy including sex.

I do want to take a quick moment to interject and just mention again the importance of what I consider my personal foundation, which was my home-based business.

Having a very strong work ethic and desire to see others thrive, grow, and succeed was literally the soil in which I was planted and could grow, in all the ways needed during my time of self-discovery.

So here I am, single and living alone, running my home-based business, and having time to do whatever I want, whenever I want, not having to answer to anyone....all the possibilities you say??? Ha ha.

I already mentioned I joined the gym so that I could be fit and healthy and have good stamina. I was working on that revenge body long before Khloe Kardashian.

And I shared that I was eating well, leafy greens on a daily basis, juicing and tons of water.

Weekends became ME time. On Sundays, when everyone else was having fun days, I'm home giving myself a facial and making sure that my skin was soft and smooth and youthful. I kept feeling the kinder I was to me, the kinder I became to others. It continued to surprise me, how the more worth I felt, the more I knew I had purpose, I mean REAL purpose, like there was plan, then I could actually be positive in others' lives and help, by if nothing else, sharing my story my life…And that feeling just kept growing.

So now I start to think, *Hey, wait a minute, I'm doing all these wonderful things but I work from home. I really only go to the grocery store once a week and the gym is certainly not a place to meet men. Way too creepy, at least for me.*

So where does a 48-year-old woman put herself, in what needs to be a target rich environment of single eligible men?

You guessed it. Online dating.

Now, let's remember that I haven't dated in almost two centuries, so it should go without saying that things have changed. I decided to throw my hat in the ring. Maybe a more experienced woman would think hey, let's try that match.com or Christian singles.

Oh no, not me, those cost money and what am I desperate????

So I decided to go with what seemed to be most popular site that costs nothing to meet singles in your area. It was called Plenty of Fish. There was also OKCupid, and let's not forget Tinder.

I do want to interrupt my flow here just to make sure that we keep this story honest and candid, so remember that you're dealing with an older woman who struggles with post-traumatic stress disorder from an abusive childhood, suffers with bouts of depression, and is about to find out just how much anxiety affects her life on an everyday basis.

Remember that right before leaving her husband, she basically had a complete and total nervous breakdown, so the building blocks are really close to the ground and the foundation is still shaky.

But like everything else in my life, I've got no time to waste and getting back to living and loving and laughing and enjoying.

I mean that's what we're here for, right??

So now my days consist of working, of course always at least ten hours a day, and taking care of myself, with the new rituals and habits like reading self-help, meditating, seeking spiritual guidance, or practicing self-care.

But believe me, none of that is as easy as it may sound. It felt like I was in a constant battle between good and evil, wanting so bad to have peace in my life, yet the abused survivor inside me didn't think I deserved it. Constantly overwhelmed with guilt for things I could've done differently and *what-iffing* myself to death. A previously mentioned, they say it takes 28 days to create a new habit, because you can't break habits. You have to create new habits in place of the old. And every time you fall off that 28 day mark you have to start all over again, so days become weeks, weeks become months, and months become years before you per-fect the self-talk and find peace and happiness in living in the moment, each moment of each new day.

But now I'm starting to sound repetitive and maybe a little philosophical, so I'll get back to the ins and outs of my daily getting-to-know-myself routine, including some of the crazy things I did, like dating men half my age or should I say boys. I am convinced that I went on more dates and kissed every frog within a 50 mile radius. I found out so quickly that I had no clue what type of man I was attracted to. I had no barometer.

It was evident that I liked a taller man as opposed to a shorter man and that I was drawn to darker hair and features commonly. But aside from that, I usually enjoyed a mans company the most when I could laugh or just feel light in the situation.

About eight months into my new normal, I met someone who had a great sense of humor and made me feel very much like a woman. We were very sexually compatible and enjoyed each other's company. But the odds were stacked against us. First off, he was eleven years younger than I was, and he had two children under the age of eight. I always promised myself that I would not get involved with a man who had minor children.

I wasn't emotionally able to give that part of myself again, nor was I willing to physically, and most importantly financially, be responsible for someone else's family. I didn't think it would be fair to them and I knew it wasn't the right thing for me. In addition to that he had a drinking problem. I'm not a snob nor am I judgmental and I actually don't have a firm understanding or belief in AA, other than I do know that sometimes it takes a village or some organized constitution for some folks to get the help and guidance that they need.

I know it had everything to do with my survival, but I just never really bought into an inability to control your actions, knowing the consequences, and allowed myself to fall victim to those types of addictions, lucky I am sure.

We dated for several months. It was nice to have a companion and someone to spend time with. We even vacationed, driving cross-country to see his kids and visit my stepmother.

But even when we were having the most fun, it was very clear to me that this was not the direction I wanted or needed to go. So it ended. Oddly enough, I didn't feel as sad as I thought I would, and although I missed the company, I refocused myself on my personal mental well-being and physical care.

And, of course, went back to dating. And dating. For the next several years that's all I did do was date and work and date some more.

I would date a lot, and then take time off, sometimes months at a time not seeing anyone, as the grueling agony of having to date men and either be rejected or disgusted was a vicious cycle and could be very draining.

The hours spent investing in getting to know someone only to find out once meeting that there was NO chemistry or that you could never see yourself with them or maybe they didn't feel an attraction to you…it was awful.

There is no way I would have ever survived this stage of life, had I not built up my self-confidence. I suppose most people have a natural progression of growth and self-worth, I was never afforded that. I was emotionally stunted as a small child and had to, (from scratch), learn how to love myself in order to love others, and to this day, I know I do it differently than most because no one ever showed me how to do it naturally. Other than the instant bound for my child, I had never had the kind of love that felt life-changing and meant something so profoundly. My love came from a place of desperation and need to feel worth, so I more "attached" myself to others and hoped they would love me and fulfill me, but that never works and I was not that person anymore.

I met some great men along the way, but for one reason or another it wasn't the right time or there were commitment issues on one side or the other. In many occasions there were children involved.

I had no idea how hard it would be to meet a man in their early 50s that didn't have children under the age of eighteen.

As months went by and turned into years, I became more comfortable just being by myself. I started to look forward to and savor those Saturdays that I would sit on the porch and drink my chai tea, reading a book or writing in a journal, or just listening to music.

I would turn up the radio, loudly playing my favorite songs anywhere from the 70s to current and dance while cleaning the house. I learned to enjoy watching movies or even sipping wine alone. And I continued with the realization that it felt good and I was happy. Now don't misunderstand me this was no epiphany. It's not like I just woke up one day and said "Gee I'm happy, how did that happen?"

. . .

I mentioned earlier, it was an inner dialogue on a daily basis, and a choice to be happy and content with my life, not needing anyone else or anything else to give me that happiness.

Many bad things happened during this time as well. In an attempt to be "friends" with my ex, I found that narcissists don't change, and that I was only getting duped into providing for that person what he needed emotionally and there was nothing in it for me. He didn't ever care about my insides and he found it easy to take advantage of me financially for years. I had to stop the internal bleeding and cut him out of my life. It was more difficult at this time in my life, because I was trying so hard to be the best person I could and I felt guilt by not always giving, but I found I had a voice and I learned to say NO.

I also had a major falling out with my daughter, who shared with me that the reason she was never having children was because of me, and that since I had had abortions in my life I should've gone ahead and aborted her as well. That was one of the most crushing if not the most crushing, heartbreaking gutting moment in my life. My heart breaks thinking and believing that I could've done something so terrible to make her feel that having children and being a parent was an awful thing.

I digress.

Even though I could find myself happy and content, over the course of those seven to eight years I was faced with much pain and many life-changing situations. Always dating, always believing, always knowing that if it was meant to be then Love would find me.

But until it did, I would enjoy crazy experiences.

Like dating a 24-year-old that for whatever reason had a role-playing fetish and liked to spend his hard money earned as a Disneyland employee buying me lingerie and fishnets. I went on what felt like a million first dates. Some I would just pay the check so I could get out of there and get home to where I now felt REAL love, love for myself, pride in building a home, decorated with MY taste, safe from any negative energy I did not want in my life.

I was a "positive" person, optimistic, kind and good towards all others. I was living a dream, did other people really feel like this? How did I truly survive all those years NOT feeling this?

I want to share it, bottle it up, give to others so the world is filled with happy people who love themselves and others freely and unabashedly.

E ven though the journey had many twists and turns, in the end I did come to the realization that I was OK by myself. And not just OK, I was great, I was happy, I was thriving.

I had forgiven everyone and everything that had ever caused me pain. I reveled in the idea that I could wake up happy and singing by myself and being alone.

I enjoyed the time I spent with my kitty cats and watering plants and all other mundane daily tasks. I had created a home for myself. I've never lived this long alone before in my entire life and I had come to a place where I had truly never been happier. Then the most unexpected thing happened.

I met him!!!

# 8

## FAIRYTALES CAN COME TRUE

I was convinced they could and hoped that they would, but had no idea what awaited me!!!

Seven years of living alone, being single, building my empire, and enjoying getting to know myself, and dare I say love myself, and becoming the happiest I could ever remember being.

I need to add that at age thirty-seven I was diagnosed with first having RRMS or Relapse and Remission Multiple Sclerosis, and secondly at forty-five, Hashimoto's disease, which is a type of hypothyroidism.

So here I am, having worked since before sixteen years of age and ultimately starting my own business. All the time struggling with my PTSD from childhood abuse and all the other abuse I suffered over the years from bad relationships and bad decisions alcohol and drug use and medical conditions, how I was even still standing was then and is still now a miracle to me.

I now know and certainly wish I had known then, that happiness is indeed an inside job.

No one, no thing, and no amount of money or material items can ever truly make you happy.

And if somebody tells you otherwise, they're not being honest.

I had built a wonderful life for myself. My home was comfy and inviting. My routine was in place. I'm very seldom overwhelmed. I enjoyed my own company and it never bothered me to be alone.

In my journey of self-discovery, I did, however, come to the conclusion at the core of it all I believed that we were created and meant to have a partner. Someone to share life with, someone to make memories with.

Often referred to as your better half or a person that completes you. I just think we were made that way.

With that said I felt I was already complete. I was happy and excited for each new day. I had some very special people in my life friends that meant the world to me and supported me in every way possible.

The downside of life was that I had no relationship with my daughter and that kept my heart broken.

I had let go of my ex completely and we had no relationship whatsoever, which was one of the healthiest things I had ever done for myself.

So here I am, looking toward my 55th birthday, not having a care in the world, happy to be alive, feeling good about myself, can't think of one thing that I need or want, and something happens to change all of that.

I met HIM.

A man that I felt more chemistry with than I have ever experienced in my lifetime.

The first time meeting was electric. I couldn't believe how much we had in common. We talked for hours, we laughed, we sang, we had deep conversation, that kind of conversation where your eyes meet and stay connected the entire time.

(I've since found out that my native American prince, with all of his old-fashioned values, believes it's important to make eye contact and keep contact during conversation.)

. . .

L et me start from the beginning and take you on the most wonderful roller coaster ride possible to the ultimate destination.

"Bliss."

So a first date turns into a morning after. (Don't judge me I'm 54 yrs old. LOL)

Breakfast in bed, and still all those amazing feelings, like I can't believe I just met this person and how can I possibly feel so connected to someone I've known less than 24 hours.

The thought of him leaving shakes me to my core. I don't want him to leave. I don't want to lose him, I want to just stay forever right now until eternity.

But that's not real life of course.

So trying to stay connected to my self-improvement path, and figure out how to let somebody into that, proved to be more difficult than one would think.

A lot of old behaviors emerged.

I'm sure I seemed a little needy at times, and it seemed that I just couldn't get enough of the energy I was experiencing, so I wanted everything now or even yesterday if that was possible when it came to time spent with this glorious man

We dated and had lots of fun trips to the movies or downtown or just the normal stuff that folks dating do, but as I mentioned, the chemistry was beyond real. I mean, within a month we were finishing each other sentences and we'd talk at length at how our connection was so strong and we didn't really even know each other but we both felt like we did maybe in another life or existence.

Now let me give you a little background on this (hard to believe he's a real man), golf pro by trade currently giving lessons to the locals in his city.

He had toured the circuit professionally but had been teaching for going on 20 years.

He was only three years younger than myself so the age difference wasn't an issue.

He did have a minor child, but the circumstances of which

were not so normal. She lived out of state and aside from that I won't mention any more as it's not my story to tell.

So I am breaking a rule. I'm falling harder than I can fathom for a man that has a child under eighteen. He's never been married.

So you scratch your head and say *Why?* I'm sure a lot of people thought that and I did hear from some, that this was a red flag.

But he was sensitive and kind and such a gentleman, always opening the door or bringing me flowers. Soft-spoken, interested in what I had to say and he listened.

I just couldn't get enough.

So I made the decision to stop dating anyone else and focus my energies on seeing what could happen with this exceptionally special man.

Well, about four months into dating, and let's not forget me putting all of my energies into it, which if you knew me personally would realize that in and of itself could be very overwhelming, because I have a lot of energy.

During the course of this time I shared my life story with him and that should scare the bejeezus out of anybody.

I mean, from being put in foster care at nine months old, to living with a stepparent whose family was chock-full of pedophiles, to suffering through the demise of that relationship, and going through more emotional and mental trauma than any child ever should, until finding themselves homeless at sixteen years old and all else that you have read about, is a lot to take in.

I shared stories of how when I was nineteen I started singing professionally and toured with some very well named bands and artists, in addition to having actual relationships with artists that became very famous.

I'm sure this guy I am dating is thinking *Who is this person? They are either completely full of crap or some type of unicorn.*

And truth be told, when I talk about my life out loud, it's very surreal, it's almost as if I hover over my body and view my life on 8 mm film.

Frame by frame, stage by stage, abusive childhood, traumatic teen years and adult life that would leave most in a gutter somewhere or six feet under.

But like I said, he always listened. He was curious yet kind, and never treated me differently or looked at me differently.

And within four months I had fallen head over heels for the 6 foot 1 Native American man.

Here we go, wait for it!!!! The proverbial ump in the road.

Oh don't say you're surprised. You had to know something would happen. This is me were talking about!!!

So it's probably safe to say that, between my hyper energy, my sense of neediness, and going all in with the *"I love you's"*, I scared the living daylights out of him.


Things then took a turn for the worse. Our communication broke down and as they say these days, he "Ghosted me."

And I found myself leaving voicemails in the middle of the night and crying, a need for closure and understanding, not getting a response.

I had to pull myself up by my bootstraps once again and convince myself that there's a reason for everything.

And even though I didn't understand, and couldn't see any possible reason there could be, after having worked so hard to get where I was both mentally and emotionally, and feeling so secure with peace in my life and my surroundings, to have something so wonderful happen but then be taken away from me so quickly really made no sense.


Well that gave way to the negative talk creeping in and becoming a daily struggle to stay positive. Luckily after a few months I was firmly back on my feet. Business was doing great, spending time with friends and enjoying that cup of chai tea on the porch with my Atkins breakfast bar put a smile on my face.

I could still see the beauty in my surroundings, one of which

I was a family of squirrels that I would buy buckets of trail mix and feed in the morning.

I also had raccoons that would visit me at night and I would leave cat food in a bowl and a bowl of water. Sometimes they would come before dark and I could get pictures. They are the silliest creatures and they made me smile and feel happy.

All of this happening in my little tiny house, in the middle of the city, in a little quiet area.

And although I would often think of all the terrible things I've gone through in my life, and of course feel the pain of my broken heart, not having any communication or a relationship with my only child, my daughter whom I love with every fiber of my being, I pressed on and I was happy because I knew it was "an inside job" and I needed to stay strong and persevere.


So you ask, what happens next? I mean I thought I had everything and clearly I don't need a man.

Well believe it or not, our skittish golf pro decided to circle back around.

After seven months of not hearing from him, not a word, not a voicemail, not a text, he called.

He wanted to know if I would be willing to give him the opportunity to sit down over dinner and try to explain what had happened, where his head was at, and allow us to have forgiveness and closure.

I wasn't immediately willing to just forget everything, but me being an empath, I was very capable of doing so.

By nature, I'm a giver, I'm a nurturer, and that is truly a blessing and a curse.

So you guessed it. Of course I agreed.

In the back of my mind I'm thinking, *Oh this guy is going to pay for what he did I mean he did break my heart after all.* That's laughable, as if I'd even know how to do that.

. . .

We agree on a day and a time, and honesty I expected myself to be nervous, but I wasn't. That was a relief. I think I had convinced myself that there was no pain that he could put upon me that I haven't felt already, and that it was up to me how little or how much I opened the door to my heart and let him back in. Wow look at me all grown up making mature decisions. That was new.

He shows up, on time of course, and in hand a dozen yellow roses. He proceeds to say that it's his understanding that yellow roses are the flower of apologies.

It doesn't hurt that yellow is my favorite color and he knew that.

We head out to dinner, to "our" spot.

Great food and the best margarita in town.

It starts out with idle chitchat. You know, how you been, what have you been up to?

If you knew me at all personally, you would know that I have the patience of a gnat, so it took me no time at all to jump right into it and ask the hard questions.

What the heck happened? What's wrong with you? Why couldn't you have just called me back when I left you a message? What did I do wrong? You said you loved me and then you just disappeared!!!

His answer was somewhat brief. He really didn't really have one, but he knew that he felt scared and a little overwhelmed. He said that he meant every word he had ever said and then he made the most profound statement.

With tears welling up in his eyes he said, "I'd like to ask you if you would be willing to give me a second chance, and allow me the next 30 years to prove to you how much I love you and what you mean to me?"

Call me crazy, call me emotional, call me whatever you want, but it didn't take .01 seconds for me to say yes.

It was almost like the seven months that had passed never

existed we spent every moment we could together after that and within six months he moved in.

We never argued or got upset with each other. Really, the transition was smooth, we spent our evenings laughing at silly television or stories from our day.

I became incredibly domestic. I would cook dinner every night and fix a cocktail for him knowing what time he would arrive since he would text me when he was leaving the golf course.

I had a singing bowl on my kitchen counter that I would ring every time he walked in the door at night.

He would get such a kick out of all the extra things I would do for him.

He would buy me flowers every week. As soon as they would start to wilt he would bring a fresh bouquet.

I showered him with golf shoes and shirts.

We went on weekend adventures to wine country or historic sites.

And even though I probably should've been afraid the entire time, waiting for that other shoe to drop and for him to disappear again, I just didn't.

And by loving him, the love for myself grow even stronger.

The love for everything in life grew stronger.

The sky became bluer, the birds chirping became louder and sweeter. The landscape of the world was so clear to me and the air was filled with hope and possibility.

Now that's not to say that I didn't ever have questions, and I am forever grateful for my friend who is a licensed marriage family therapist who was there for me to listen to whatever I had to say when we met at the gym twice a week.

She was a saving grace for sure and I will never forget what she did for me during that time and how she supported me and gave me strength to see the positive and the good at all times!!! Go Team Rick, she would say. Thanks SJR

. . .

For the most part, we settled in like an old married couple and 13months into the new relationship on one of our weekend adventures to a mountain cabin he popped the question.

And with tears in both our eyes I said yes again.

If you thought it was good before, boy did it get even better.

I know people will argue that love isn't a picnic. Or all butterflies and rainbows, and that's true. But what it can be is amazing.

It was gentle and kind, supportive and loving, understanding and interesting also motivating and satisfying.

Of course we've had trials and tribulations.

After much discussion and looking toward the future, we made the decision to move out of California.

And although leaving California was difficult, especially since Richard, being a golf pro, needed the sunshine and golf courses to make a living. We took a huge leap of faith moving to the country, not knowing what to expect, and just having faith that all we had in life that was positive and being who we were that only good could happen.

Unfortunately that's not what happened, albeit there was one bright spot over the course of the next eight months and that was us becoming man and wife.

Aside from that we were once again subject to a great deal of emotional abuse, verbal abuse, and hate.

We did everything that was necessary to stay positive. To find happy in each day and try to figure out what to do next, as we were stuck or at least we felt that way temporarily.

But almost like Power Rangers, we activated everything we had inside ourselves and decided to find somewhere to move again so that we could have the space and positive energy in our environment to figure out the next fork in our path.

. . .

All in all honestly we created none of the negativity ourselves it was more circumstances of choices made based on trust and commitment of others.

They say no good deed goes on punished.

I guess that was a lesson we had to learn again! Hope it sticks!!


At the end of the day, we have no regrets. Everything we've done, every decision we've made, every promise that was broken by others, has only made us stronger.

Now, over three years later, we still giggle on a daily basis, smile up to the sky grateful for how we've been blessed with what we have. We ache for how sad it must be because not everyone in life is able to share an experience of love that's filled full of laughter and contentment.

Having a home-based business, we spend almost all of our time together and I can't imagine it any other way.

He is my absolute everything. Not like another half or my better half, nor does he complete me. He is the air that I breathe every day.

Sometimes I say "Well I had a hard life. I went through a lot, I deserve this happiness."

However, those types of statements only make me feel guilty when I know that so many others want and don't have it.


So I say this instead:

I've gone through the fire and suffered for that which I do not know why.

I've worked hard and struggled to have what I've now been given.

And in loving myself was able to love others more.

No one should ever have to experience abuse of any kind,

and I wouldn't wish the life I had to live on another human being.

With that said.

If this is how it ends, blissfully happy and totally in love and capable of sustaining a life in today's society, then as they say "it's all worth it" right?

I don't know, I don't have all the answers and I never said that I did and I would never say that I do.

What I do know is that being positive and having an open, loving heart and an open mind to learn and grow, and most importantly an ability to accept everyone and everything around you exactly as it is, surrendering to a higher power, has brought joy to my life.

The kind of joy that makes your heart feel like it's going to burst right out of your chest.

The kind of joy that upon awakening every morning you smile, not even knowing why.

Acceptance is the key to learning that life and love is and always will be: AN INSIDE JOB!!!!

# ABOUT THE AUTHOR

Born in Southern California in 1962.

A lover of life and love from the beginning.

My first being my beautiful daughter Aleah Breanne, who is forever in my heart.

And now my one true romantic love, my husband Rich.

Through all my ups and downs I have been blessed and will forever be grateful for this journey.

May my words somehow touch the souls so full of the pain of the past and give light to the future.